Personal Growth Through Copier Sales

Carl Nelson

ISBN:0692330402
ISBN-13:9780692330401

DEDICATION

Much gratitude to my Producer, Linda Jordan and Wife, Lynn.

Plays by Carl Nelson:
Into the Wild Blue Yonder
Personal Growth Through Copier Sales
Ollie's Day Out

Essays by Carl Nelson:
The Audience is a Mob

Poetry by Carl Nelson:
A Poet's Past Lives
Shoving My Way Into the Conversation

All are currently available through Amazon books.

CONTENTS

ACKNOWLEDGMENTS

PERSONAL GROWTH THROUGH COPIER SALES was first produced as a One Act, "The Great Chain of Being", in Theatre Babylon's Nine Holes Rises From the Ashes New Works Festival. This short play became Scene One of the full length play, SAVING HARRY - which was later produced by Linda Jordan and opened June 16th, 2006 at the Youngstown Cultural Arts Center, West Seattle, in the Thelma DeWitty Theater. Director was Irv Zimmer. Stage Manager was G. S. Haupert. Set/Lighting/Sound Designer was Alex Wren. Assistant Producer was Lynn Nelson. Charles Brastrup played Harry Coombs. Sam Tregoning played Bobby Mayfair. Daniel Wood played Claude Gustafson. Nick Cameron played Louis Aargon. And Scot Bastian played Jerry Harken.

Many thanks also, to the donors who personally and collectively made this production possible.

PERSONAL GROWTH THROUGH COPIER SALES

CHARACTERS:

Harry Coombs....... legendary copier salesperson, 60
Claude Gustafson.... Harry's interim helper, former poet
Bobby Mayfair........ Near Eastern immigrant salesperson
Jerry Harken.......... salesperson
Louis Aargon......... VP of Marketing

PERSONAL GROWTH THROUGH COPIER SALES

ACT ONE

STARRING! "... the cold, relentless, insatiable, furious spirit of commerce."

- Valerie Martin

TIME: Over a four month period.

SETTING: The office of a moderately-sized branch copier sales dealership.

One key aspect of a copier sales dealership is that even though the company has been here for years, the office furniture, phones, computers could easily be removed in a few hours leaving just another block of raw office space. In fact, several of the salespeople, who have been working here for months, still have their stuff in cardboard boxes. Many of the occupied cubicles are quite messy. And none of the vacated cubicles have been cleaned up. Abandoned articles of former salespeople rest gathering dust. Their photos of family, favorite boats and cars, and vacations still haunt the walls. A wad of gum sitting on a wrapper gathers dust. The hustle of work flows around all of this. The vacant littered cubicles are like tombstones in a sales village…

Prominently hung is a large white board with all of the salespersons named according to the sales team. After each name are their sales figures for the current month. These figures will change. Sixty thousand would generally be an adequate month; anything over eighty, a good month; anything under forty, a weak month; anything like ten or fifteen… start scrounging for a cardboard box.

Prior to lights up, the sounds of a busy sales bullpen fill the darkened theater. CLAUDE sits in a cubicle chair across from where HARRY COOMBS will sit. HARRY has recently suffered a right-side stroke, which, while it doesn't affect his verbal ability, affects the motor capability to the left side of his body. He has to wipe drool from his lip occasionally, walks with a slight limp, bumps into things he doesn't perceive, and tires easily.

AT RISE: CLAUDE sits nervously as HARRY enters.

SCENE 1

HARRY: So you're Claude, the poet, …and proud new father.

CLAUDE: Yes sir.

HARRY: You have your father's smile. Bill always had a good smile.

CLAUDE: Thanks.

HARRY: So why is it you want to be in sales Claude?

CLAUDE: Well, I've had a little practice helping my wife out, and I found it got me out of the doldrums.

HARRY: (frowns) Sales involves a lot of rejection.

CLAUDE: Yes, but it's the science of understanding and overcoming it!
Whereas with poetry, when people reject you, you dig deeper into yourself. Then they reject that. So you dig deeper. After a while, you're so removed from your audience that they don't even feel the

tiny rumble as the shoring collapses, and your voice is lost forever.
Why, they're probably having a picnic miles above at that very time, on that very site... in the bright sunshine. At best, the little tremble in the earth as you're lost forever? ...it adds a little mystery to their lives... a frisson.
        (a beat)
All they agree upon is, you were looking a little wild-eyed there, towards the end!

HARRY: Okay.

CLAUDE: It's a fascinating situation, really.
Telemarketing is a lot like writing a poem. ...only instead of having to conjure those damned voices, you're given their phone number.

HARRY: Uh... huh?

CLAUDE: When you think of how hard it is to actually have real relationships? It's a very exciting situation, really! A complete stranger practically breathing, right into your ear...
 (earnestly) I have no idea of how the world was then, that is, when you were my age. But, you know, now, everybody TALKS about how alienated everyone is? All the while, there it is... the phone!
Right under my nose! (sighs) ...all these years.

HARRY: So you've given up poetry for... telemarketing?

CLAUDE: I don't think of it as telemarketing so much as moving up The Great Chain of Being: as the Reincarnation of my poetry.
Something doesn't work? You arise from the ashes of that, like a Phoenix.

HARRY: Like a… Phoenix.

CLAUDE: (nods) The Mythical Bird!
It used to be - as a Poet, you know - it was all THEM ...the voices, yammering, yammering, yammering. I was ready to line my hat with tinfoil!

(very serious)

Now, every day! I'm making headway. I've got their damned number.

HARRY: Well... like I say, that's great.
That's fine.

(a beat)

So how are you with poems that... hang up.

CLAUDE: Ha! Poets deal with that all the time.

HARRY: Ha!

CLAUDE: Rejection is mother's milk to me.

HARRY: ...that's great.

CLAUDE: However, it is still a big stretch from this poetic focus of mine on the accumulation of wisdom through mortification of the ego - a 'play of passion' as it were - to the actual achievement of success.
I know how to broaden my sense of Self through failure. But this idea of personal growth through achievement and success in the world. I have to admit, it has me fascinated.

(a beat)

Plus, I do need the money. So, you know, 'we take risks'.

HARRY: Well then, we're on the same page for sure.
It's probably something you can't see, having been an introverted, self-involved, totally wrapped up in himself artist... but it's something the salesperson knows, having been out and about and done commerce with the world. Life is not entirely failure. It's just MOSTLY failure. So, it's just a numbers game. You keep up your activity, and your success is virtually assured.

CLAUDE: Really?

HARRY: Really.

CLAUDE: I'll tell my friends.

HARRY: I'm sure your will.
    (a beat)
But you screw this up and you're history.

CLAUDE: Gee, the chance of getting fired! The way you describe it, in a strange way, it's relaxing. You see, with poetry, you just keep going... and going. No one tells you, "For God's sakes, stop!"

    (a beat)

HARRY: You know, frankly? You're a little... bizarre.
    (a beat)
But the fact is, I need somebody with phone skills and the word is, out on the street, that you have the chops.
Tell you what! Right now.
We'll role play.

CLAUDE: (shifting forward, eye to eye) You know this is really something I like about sales... this sense of conversational sport.

    (HARRY faces the audience, and places hand to ear as if taking a call.)

CLAUDE: Because I am not really interested in business, in the way a businessman is. I am more interested in business as an outgrowth of how vigorous conversation is actually structured.

HARRY (wiggling his phone hand)

CLAUDE: Right.
    (facing audience)
And so, it occurred to me, that Sales defines the 'leading edge' of any endeavor! You take poetry - or any sort of writing, or Art for that matter - and as soon as the fledgling artist begins to make money, that is, selling... it's "Goodbye, school!" Except for actors ironically, who realize that good acting IS sales.

(HARRY indicates he should 'get to it'.)
(CLAUDE nods, puts hand to ear, dials.)
Hello?

HARRY: Hello?

CLAUDE: Good morning, may I speak with Harry Coombs?

HARRY: (bruskly) This is Harry Coombs.

CLAUDE: Hi Harry.
        (quickly mirrors HARRY's diction and pacing)
This is Claude Gustafson at Better Business Systems in Carbondale? We handle copiers, printers, and fax machines. And I had spoken briefly with Curtis Black, who apparently is your IT ("I-tee")fellow? who said that you would be the one to speak with regarding the purchase and leasing of such equipment at your company?

HARRY: Yes, that's the case. But I have to tell you before you go any further that we are already in a long term arrangement with a local firm that has served our needs well for many years, and we are not looking to make a change at this time.

CLAUDE: Actually Harry, my wife worked for many years at another copier dealership. So, I know what you mean about having long term, loyal customers! We had many! of those. And they often came to us with much the same dilemma.

HARRY: Dilemma?

CLAUDE: Some salesperson - you know, some sharp up-and-comer - has been quite persistent and nice, and they felt like they ought to give them a hearing. Plus, what if their boss looked at the offer and asked, "This is the best price we can get?" So. They felt it would always look good to the higher ups, if they got more than one bid.

        (a beat)

CLAUDE: What could we say? We always did the right thing! We told them "by all means hear the fellow out!" And things went from there.
>   (a beat)
What do you say, Harry?

HARRY: I'd say, it's been very nice talking with you.
But I don't see you coming over. And I don't see us switching.
>   (laughs)
And I see things going from there.

CLAUDE: (says nothing)

>   (a long beat)

HARRY: We've been with the same vendor for going on ten years now.

>   (a beat)

HARRY: (hinting) We haven't shopped the market in a long time...?

>   (a beat)

HARRY: Because there's been no need! They have handled our needs well, and we've been satisfied.
 (listening to other hand) And they look out after your interests?
(speaking into first hand) You could say so. We think we've been well-served.
(listening to other hand) And has an audit of your current and projected document flow been performed within the last two years so that you know exactly where you stand in terms of per copy cost, and employee downtime?

>   (CLAUDE says nothing.)

HARRY: (yelling into first hand) Aren't you going to say a blasted

7

thing?

CLAUDE: What is it you would like me to say, Harry?

HARRY: What?

CLAUDE: Most of the people I speak with Harry, once they've stated their position as emphatically as yours, hang up.

HARRY: Is that what you're waiting for? For me to hang up?

CLAUDE: Mr. Coombs, may I be frank?

HARRY: You can be Santa Claus! I just wish we could end this.

CLAUDE: You sound like a man trapped in an unhealthy marriage.

(a beat)

HARRY: Marriage?

CLAUDE: You see your business situation very clearly, but you don't see anything you can do about it.

HARRY: I have been successfully married for ...over thirty years! And we have a current vendor, like I said.
            (HARRY thinks.)
And he is my brother-in-law!

CLAUDE: And...
Do you like your brother-in-law?

HARRY: Like? Garth? (a beat) What's to like?

CLAUDE: (empowering) Because I have the feeling that your brother-in-law has been taking advantage of your relationship, and that you would like to do something about it. And THAT's why you're speaking with me. Because you are holding out some hope, beyond all hope, that I might be able to bring something to the table, that I might offer you some options...

HARRY: Hey, if you can see any blue sky in this situation?
	(laughing)
What are you selling... a divorce?

CLAUDE: How about we meet Tuesday, at 11:15? And I'll tell you.

HARRY: Right, Mr. Smartass. And would you like me to bring my wife and my brother-in-law?

CLAUDE: If it wouldn't be too much to ask?

HARRY: (smiling) Really? Because they are here, right now, listening.

CLAUDE: Great, and I'm in the area! Why don't I drop by?

HARRY: You haven't the balls.

CLAUDE: I can be there in a half hour.

HARRY: Okay, hot shot. We'll be ready.

CLAUDE: By the way Harry, could you put together a list of your current equipment, and have copies of your current leasing agreements made in the meanwhile?

	(Staring at each other.)

	(BOTH hang up.)

HARRY: (nodding) You kind of got my goat there.

CLAUDE: I'm sorry.

HARRY: (weighing CLAUDE) So you like sales chatter?

CLAUDE: I enjoy it very much.

    (a beat)

HARRY: So do I.
You can probably tell this is a very active place. We do a lot of selling. It can get quite loud. Lots of chatter. That's what we do. Kind of like a fast game of pick-up basketball. You play any sports, Claude?

CLAUDE: No. But I'd like to.

HARRY: You'd like to? What's the matter with you? You sick?

CLAUDE: No.

    (a beat)

HARRY: You're kind of a listener, a spectator, aren't you?

CLAUDE: I suppose so.

HARRY: Real salespeople are always moving, always selling.

    (HARRY dribbles and feints with bad hand, passing the ball to CLAUDE suddenly with his good arm.)

    (CLAUDE jerks.)

HARRY: But… you're kind of a ninja on the phone.
Tell you what we'll do. We'll have you work the phones as planned. But every morning when we meet here to record appointments, I want you to sell me. Doesn't matter what. Maybe just that today is the best day of the year, no question! But I want you to close me. Think you can do that?

CLAUDE: Maybe I could call? Set an appointment, instead?

HARRY: Maybe look at it this way. I'm the boss.

CLAUDE: I hope I'm up to this.

HARRY: (wiping lip) Claude, you just voiced the veteran salesperson's first thought of the day.

SCENE 2

SETTING: Same. A week later.

(CLAUDE is talking into the phone at his desk.)

CLAUDE: (earnestly) So Raphael, I'd thought that maybe, even with my poetical - maybe even because! of my poetical nature - I could be of help.
My wife, of course, leapt at the opportunity. She furnished me with a long list of places to call, and with a script of what to say. It sounded sort of 'canned'. 'Can you really talk to people like this?' I thought. "You really say this?" But as it turned out. She was right, and I was wrong. Not only could you talk to people like that, but they responded. Let me tell you; it changed my life. Or, at least, it should have. I mean, it LOOKS like it SHOULD BE changing my life. The fact that it hasn't changed my life, I hold only myself to blame. I still

can't seem to grasp …something …whatever it is.

(HARRY enters limping.)

CLAUDE: But, look Raphael, I've got to go. Here's the deal. You get us in to see… Stan, the Firm Administrator, and I promise you ten minutes this Friday evening at the Open Mike.
    (a beat)
Okay then. See you. But Sandy over at Concrete Products is wanting that spot too.
…So give me a call!

(HARRY looks around his desk, picks up a scrap of paper.)

HARRY: (reading)
    "In the green pond by the mossy weir,
     the flowering lotus blossom attests:
     Today is the best day of the year,
     no question."

(HARRY looks at CLAUDE.)

CLAUDE: (smiling) Good morning, Harry.

HARRY: Good morning..
    (tries to pick and shuffle through his "to do" stack, but the papers slip through his weak grip and scatter across the floor)
Any appointments for me?

CLAUDE: (helping to pick them up) Just two.
    (handing HARRY the appointments)

HARRY: Well, keep on it. And I've got a doctor's appointment downtown at one. Should last about an hour.

CLAUDE: Okay. I'll try to schedule you around it.

HARRY: …Damn it.
    (tries to pick a pen with his left hand)

CLAUDE: What?

HARRY: (embarrassed) Try not to schedule me too tight. It looks like I'm still getting my wings.

CLAUDE: Okay. How are you feeling?

HARRY: Still a little unsteady.

CLAUDE: I suppose these things take time.

HARRY: (fumbling again) I suppose.

CLAUDE: You want a hand?

HARRY: No. I want the whole other half of my body! You got one you don't need?

CLAUDE: (silence)

HARRY: Sales rule number one. Don't offer something you don't have. Don't promise something you can't provide. It's incredible around here how often that rule is broken. If I ever hear you lying on the phone, you're out of here. You got that?

CLAUDE: Yes sir.

HARRY: And it's not sir, it's Harry. You're Claude, and I'm Harry. Nobody's going to be persuaded by anybody but an equal.
    (a beat, as HARRY takes a long breath)
So. Claude. How's the business climate this morning?

CLAUDE: "Today's the best day of the year, no question."

HARRY: Let's hope not.
Here. I've got some more call lists here that you can start on. But before we get to that, there's a list of my... our, current customers

whose leases are coming due within a year. I need an appointment with each of them. Look to see who signed off on the lease. That's the person I want to meet with.

(CLAUDE nods.)

(HARRY trying to type.)

HARRY: And these e mails. Why can't people use the blasted ...phone anymore?

CLAUDE: You want me to type the answer?

HARRY (sighs) I suppose you'll have to. You're a writer, correct? We might as well put you to use.

CLAUDE: Our computers are synced.

HARRY: Okay, here's one. Can you read that?

(HARRY opens e mail.)

CLAUDE: (reading) "Harry. How are you doing? Heard you're back at work. Can you get me that software upgrade by tomorrow? - Stan"

HARRY: Type: "Stan. Thanks for asking. Skip still has a hitch, but am well into my recovery. Will get that software to you today. - Harry"
Got that?

CLAUDE: Yeah.

HARRY: (leans back, tired.) Okay, send it.

CLAUDE: It's sent.

HARRY: (trying to sit up) Good. One down. Two, and we're on a roll. What's next?

CLAUDE: Let's see.
       (reading, and bothered)
Here's one from... "Tom"?

HARRY: Yeah. Tom Skanzi, at Skanzi Mortgage and Loan. I'll open that later.

       (lights out)

SCENE 3

SETING: Same, a week later.

HARRY: (holding a printed e mail)

>"In the green pool where the frog squats,
>   his meal approaches.
>   This is the best day of the year,
>   no question."

Reads kind of like a poem.

CLAUDE: It's a Haiku.

HARRY: That's nice.

CLAUDE: It means… that I'm hard at work over here! That I sense
deals! approaching. It's about closing.
It's meant to be a positive message.

HARRY: Do you know what it means to me?
It means that being practical is a challenge for you.

CLAUDE: I hadn't thought of it that way.

HARRY: (nodding at e-mail) Yes, that practicality is like some
elusive colored bird to you, flitting here and there…

CLAUDE: (caught by the idea) That's true.

HARRY: …creating some glimmering, glistening, nonsensical path.

CLAUDE: It's mesmerizing.

HARRY: That's not how it works.

CLAUDE: It's not?

HARRY: No. Practical things don't "flit about". Fantasies! do.
Practical things, (smacks desk with his cane), they stay put.

CLAUDE: !

HARRY: (threatening) They do. In fact, it seems to be the very
NATURE of practical objectives - that they have to be sought after.
You know what they say about gold? That it's "where you find it?"
        (CLAUDE nods)
Well, "find" is the operative word.
        (wiggles hand to ear, like a phone)
You have to go looking!

CLAUDE: Yes, but shouldn't you get prepared first?   Like with
pack animals and such?

        (HARRY stares.)

HARRY: Claude. Let me ask you this: 'If you had a Zillion! dollars,
what would you do?'

CLAUDE: Well. It would certainly give me pause to think.

HARRY: (sighs) That's what I thought.

CLAUDE: (pointing) But then again, I see your point! For if "gold
is where you find it", then what do you need to know, or CAN you
know, for certain? Gee, that's weird. You just start.
Being 'practical' - is about the most IMpractical thing in the world!

HARRY: Anyway you can get your head around it.

CLAUDE: So…

(HARRY indicates CLAUDE should pick up the phone and start calling.)

CLAUDE: (nodding) This is what makes it so great! We just want them to buy a copier.

HARRY: That's right.

CLAUDE: And we leave it at that.

HARRY: Sounds good.

CLAUDE: It's straightforward. It's honest. And it's like such a relief! It's all about words FINALLY being effective. I know where the conversation is going - and they know where the conversation is going.
(a beat)
And you know something else this has all taught me, Harry?

HARRY: I don't. want. to know, Claude.

CLAUDE: It's the power, of the simple. declarative. sentence, Harry.

HARRY: Get to work.

CLAUDE: (nodding) There you are!
(picking up the phone)
This whole business is built around the power of the simple declarative sentence. People WANT to be told what to do. They NEED to be told what to do.

HARRY: Dial the phone!

CLAUDE: (nods) I mean, I need to be told what to do!
(waving phone)
And this is the area, as a poet, where I feel I have made my biggest conceptual advance. (dialing) "Less is More," Harry. As a poet, I had been saying entirely too much. Here, I can see that by concentrating

my efforts on a few singular statements, and by repeating these few singular sentences ritualistically... You simply refine until each word flows like water - and yet hits like a brick! Until finally, your verbal Presence is so Immense that all Opposition collapses with just a...

VOICE on phone: Vanderberg, Johnson and Bailey.

CLAUDE: (striking forward) "Hello!"

SCENE 4

SETTING: Same, later that day.

> (BOBBY is talking on his cell phone while pacing before
> CLAUDE's cubicle.)

BOBBY: Yeah. Yeah. I know I said that, but listen. Here is even
better deal.
> (a beat)
Yeah. Yeah. I know. I know. But you haven't heard better deal.
Okay. Here it is. Here is better deal. We swap you machine which
will do what you want for machine you have.
I know. I know. But I go to boss, and I say, just what you said. And
he says, you know how bosses are... So I say again to him, just what
I said I said before... and this time, I see little daylight there, I think.
So next time around I say just what I said before, only this time I add
just a little.   And anyway, to make long story short, I work the
problem hard, believe me! But it's good, because now I think I can
give you this even better deal, you see?
You want to hear better deal?
> (listens, shaking head)
(petulant)   Okay.   Now you being bad customer, you know?
Because, like I say, I work very hard...
> (listens, nods)
Okay. Okay, so this is better deal...
> (BOBBY sees LOUIS enter and walks out of
> earshot)
 (giggles) Actually, you know, this mistake not such a bad thing - for
you, anyway. As it's the first time I see the boss go this far on deal.
He usually pretty tight. But anyway, here is deal...

LOUIS: So how's Harry doing?

CLAUDE: Pretty well, I think.

LOUIS: He's able to meet all his appointments?

CLAUDE: More or less. If there's a problem, I re-schedule.

LOUIS: You re-schedule?
It's tough. I can imagine, losing control over half of my body at the age of 60. Not that far from retirement, and then this.

CLAUDE: He's tough.

LOUIS: You don't have to tell me that.
        (LOUIS is speaking loud enough so that the surrounding
        salespeople overhear.)
I ever tell you how Harry took me out on one of my first appointments?
        (looking up)
...Where, does the time, go?
        (LOUIS glances about.)
I was just a young buck full of piss and vinegar. Lots of energy. I could run the hundred in under ten flat. And I knew damned well even then, that I had no interest in getting a job, just so that some old FART in a new SUIT could tell me what to do. When, all of a sudden, we were driving lickety split down this hill and Harry yells, (in HARRY's absolutely commanding voice) "Stop the car!"
(nods) So I stopped.
        (no laughter)
        (LOUIS laughs loudly, and indicates they should.)
        (some laughter)
        (LOUIS laughs more loudly and more aggressively)
        (more laughter)
        (LOUIS laughs even more loudly and aggressively while
        aiming his attentions as those who are holding back.)
        (great laughter all around)
        (LOUIS smiles.)
Harry had been trying to get back in to see this client, who he fears is about to reneg on a verbal agreement, because he doesn't take Harry's calls. And so, as Harry sees him get out of his car, he points

him out to me. And then, it's like we're cops, chasing a perp. Except that we're carrying our sight sellers and day timers. And we haven't gone more than fifty feet, when the guy turns around and catches sight of Harry! And you should have seen the look on his face.

So I run in this one door, while Harry goes after him through another. And I'm thinking all along, as I run after this guy, 'this is sales?'

But we head the guy off just as he steps from the elevator. Where Harry grins! just as friendly as you please.

"Hi Tom. Glad I caught you!" Harry says. And then Harry pulls out his famous pen, and produces the paperwork...

The guy up and signs it, right there.

(catching the eye of surrounding salespeople)

That's when you realize this game is different. This isn't about sitting behind a desk! It's about bird-dogging! and flushing them out.

(a beat, as the salespeople scatter for their coats)

Harry taught me a lot! Anything he says, you listen!

(LOUIS turns his attention back to CLAUDE.)

So. How's he selling?

CLAUDE: I can't tell you. I'm making the appointments. After that, it's off my radar.

LOUIS: He hasn't mentioned having you go out?

CLAUDE: He's thinking about having ME, go out?

LOUIS: He told me, one of the reasons this stroke of his wasn't going to be a problem, was that he was getting an assistant. So that if it got too hectic, you could fill in.

(a beat)

He didn't tell you?

He said that you were seasoned, and had experience...

CLAUDE: He just said, I should wear a tie.

(LOUIS nods, and leaves.)

(BOBBY and JERRY collect around CLAUDE after

LOUIS leaves.)

BOBBY: So. You're new guy

JERRY: What's your name?

BOBBY : Claude. I already know. This guy is Claude.

JERRY : Is that right?

BOBBY: Yeah, that right. I say so, didn't I?

JERRY: (ignoring CLAUDE's outstretched hand) Alright then, you know so much. Tell me how much Harry is paying him.

BOBBY: How much is Harry paying you? Yeah. Fine.
          (shakes CLAUDE's hand)
C'mon. Go ahead. You can tell us.

JERRY: You really think Harry's going to let him tell us?

BOBBY: So already, you do everything Harry says? You are... what they call it? ...a froggie!

JERRY: A toady.

BOBBY: Right. A toadie.
Okay. So we do it this way. Is he paying you ...ten dollar an hour?

          (BOTH looking closely at CLAUDE.)

BOBBY: No?

JERRY: Yes?

JERRY: It's got to be more than ten dollars an hour, you cheap bastard.

BOBBY: I'm not saying I pay him ten dollars an hour!

I'm saying, maybe how much is Harry paying?
      (BOTH watch as... CLAUDE says nothing.)
(to JERRY) He got pretty good poker face, you know?
(to CLAUDE) All you have to say is "yes or no". You don't have to say what it is.

JERRY: So you can hire him away.

BOBBY: So why you want to know so bad yourself? You not doing so good this month, huh?

JERRY: I'm doing fine.

BOBBY: This month is tough? Everybody having a hard time this month. Is not big deal to admit it.

JERRY: Read my lips, "I'm doing fine." And maybe you'd do better yourself, if you tried learning the language.

BOBBY: Hey, I know language. I know language real good. Is language of sales. You heard of that, maybe? Perhaps you heard? Language of ...selling things!

JERRY: So how much IS Harry paying you?

      (CLAUDE is silent.)

BOBBY: Ah, he toadie. He can't say. Harry no let him speak to us. But. If he not paying you over ten dollar and hour, you being robbed. Big time!
That is, if you any good. You any good? I hear you pretty good?

JERRY: Of course he's good. You think Harry would hire anybody who wasn't good?
(to CLAUDE) If he's not giving you a percentage of the leads you give him, you're getting robbed you know. A base pay of ten dollars an hour is nothing!

BOBBY: If you any good I not pay you anything an hour! You know why?

Why, is because I give you 50%, half of everything. Oh, and we clean up. We make boatloads.

JERRY: Half?

BOBBY: What's the matter? You not hear so good? I say,
        (shaping mouth to say distinctly)
…"Halff".

JERRY: What I thought I heard you say was, "haaalllf".

BOBBY: Sure! I say, "halllf". Half, hallf, hallllf! What's the matter with you?

JERRY: He's either lying or out of his mind. Nobody does a straight split for leads.

BOBBY: I not lying and I not out of my mind. What I am, is CLOSER.
I can do this because when you bring me deal, I close.
So. Right away, I make half of everything you do. Is all gravy, you see. You should work for me.
So what he pay you? Ten dollar an hour is peanut.

JERRY: That's "peanuts".

BOBBY: Don't tell me how much it is. I know! …peanut.
(to CLAUDE) I give you nothing but commission, and we both get rich.
You want get rich don't you?
        (a beat)
You not want to get rich?

JERRY: He's a poet! And he's got a new kid.
That's why he's here. That's why he's working for Harry.

BOBBY: How you know all this? Nobody tell me anything. Is this true? You are …a poet?

CLAUDE: Well, yes! But as I was telling Harry, I have this idea that SALES, really defines the 'leading edge' of ANY endeavor? Plus, the idea of personal growth through the achievement of SUCCESS in the world, really fascinates me. (nodding) So...

JERRY: (ignoring what CLAUDE has said) The thing you need to know about Bobby is to only believe half of what he says.
(to BOBBY) I take that back. It's closer to around... five percent.

BOBBY: Why you talk like that to new employee?

JERRY: It's because, he's new.

BOBBY: I not say bad things about you. Have I said anything bad about him? You want me to say bad things about you?

JERRY: Go ahead. I'd like to hear it.

BOBBY: Okay. He's cheap.

JERRY: Cheap?

BOBBY: When you give me anything?

JERRY: Give you something?

BOBBY: Why, even to get a "Good Morning" out of him, is tough. Nothing. He give away nothing free.

JERRY: Well excuse me. "Good morning." There.

BOBBY: Is afternoon already. (to CLAUDE) You see how he pay you, always late too! you work for him?
Plus, he can't close.

JERRY: Can't close? Bullshit!
Who closed the Sherry Foods account just last month? And Balley Construction. (counting on fingers) and Gillian Architecture, and ...

BOBBY: You lost Better Builders.

JERRY: I did not lose Better Builders. Better Builders decided to buy off the Internet. Better Builders wanted me to pay them. Better Builders thought they could buy 3 copiers plus scanning and all the chrome, right from the factory, software and all, get it installed and up and running without any relationship to a dealer at all. I told them I'd be here when they came to their senses "i.e." need service! They should be calling me... (checking watch) ...any time now.

BOBBY: They not call you. They call someone else. And you know why? Because you make them look bad. You arrogant. And that why you not know how to close.

JERRY: Close a deal that's going to cost ME money? (to CLAUDE) You see why he claims he can close anything? Be smart. Whatever you do, don't work off him for commission.

BOBBY: It's a lie. Off every deal I make money.

JERRY: Green cheese. He's selling you green cheese.

BOBBY: Clean grease? Green peas? You know another reason he can't sell is, no one know what the hell he is talking about. Plus, he talk too fast.
Hey! You want to close? Maybe you learn the language. You know? So people understand you better!
(to CLAUDE) So what you say? You want to come work for me?

        (HARRY enters.)

        (JERRY warns BOBBY as he spots HARRY approaching.)

BOBBY: (turns) Harry! So how you doing?
        (BOBBY holds up his hand to indicate he has incoming call on his 'blue tooth'.)
Oh! Got to take call.
        (BOBBY scurries off.)

27

JERRY HARKEN: Harry! So here's the deal.
>   (trying to get it all in very quickly, in the time HARRY shuffles
>   across the stage)
He NEEDS equipment! Lots of equipment. And he wants it networked of course, plus duplexing, scanning, the whole package plus speed, lots of speed; because that's one of their biggest bugaboos. They literally can't keep up with the demand for paper flow; it's that crazy! Just let me continue.
And I'm not talking to the office manager, or the IT fellow about all this. I'm talking to the Owner, himself. His name's Clive. Clive Barrow. He's British. But as fate would have it, he grew up two blocks from my old home!
So we're like tight. We're really tallying up the needs, and benefits. And I'm doing a good job. Not piling on the chrome or anything. Just a well thought out, thorough analysis. If anything, it's the CUSTOMER – and I mean the MAIN MAN here - asking for more! Ask Mike, because I had him in on this too. Because they ALSO need lots of color! I mean, it's like this copier salesman's beautiful technicolor dream! So then I go to the leasing company. Just let me continue, please!
And the leasing company turns me down flat!

HARRY: What he wanted was for you to find the financing for him.

JERRY This is a business that provides sterilized blister-packaging, for Godsakes!
>   (HARRY frowns.)
Extends the shelf-life for years! Just do the research. It's going to be humoungous. And if I presently had the financial liquidity, I'd invest in it myself.
>   (a beat)
So I go to Donovan, and I say, "Donovan, if we can put together the financing, we can do this deal - he wants to wrap this deal by the END OF THIS MONTH - and it's big!"

HARRY: So this Owner, this "Clive", he's created quite a sense of urgency in you?

JERRY: What I am doing is trying to create some "sense of urgency" in Donovan! For goodness sakes, Harry? To light a fire, of some sort.

HARRY: The man has an asbestos ass.

JERRY: No kidding. So then I said, "Donovan, everything is already done. All WE have to do is arrange the FINANCING."   And he raises up, so abruptly that he completely misses the ball!
        (Harry laughs.)
"No!" I said. "Let me clarify! He is financially very sound. He just hasn't any credit! - at this. particular. point in time. This is a growing business! perched to go virtually ballistic. Do you realize how important shelf-life is to the perishable products industry?"
And… it's like he doesn't care.
        (HARRY shakes his head, smiling.)
        (JERRY moves to stand in HARRY's path.)
"Donovan", I tell him. "I've got a zillion signed orders here, amounting to over FIVE hundred thousand dollars - DOable by the END OF THIS CURRENT MONTH. Do you think you could interrupt your golf game for just ONE second?"

HARRY: You actually stood between Donovan and the hole?

JERRY: Sorry. (moving out of HARRY's way)   I kind of put that in there as a rhetorical flourish. But, … darn it! That's what's wrong with this place. Not that I'm down on golf, or anything.

HARRY: (nods)

JERRY: But who around here has their eye on the ball? Just give me one name. Just give me one name of someone around here who I can go to, who actually has the power to get something done, who actually WILL work to get something done, and I will go there.

HARRY: You talk to Louis?

JERRY: To do that I would have to go over Donovan's head.
You think we should go over Donovan's head on this?

HARRY: We?

JERRY: Hey, we're on the same team here. You know, working the problem. You always see things so clearly.
(a beat)
All I'm asking is for a little of your expertise. You know, with Louis. You've been around here, a long time.
(following)
Louis knows you, and what's more he trusts! you, Harry.

HARRY: So that's what you want from me here. You want me to squeeze Louis.

JERRY: No Harry, that's not it at all!

HARRY: And you want it for free.

JERRY: I'm not against a split, if it should come to that.

HARRY: (turns, smiles)

JERRY: I'm just saying that just like I would get a HUGE commission if I were to make this sale. Likewise I could see my way clear to give you something if you were to help me to secure the sale, with Louis.
(a beat)
You get Louis to okay this deal, and it's an equal split.
What do you say?

HARRY: It seems to me that if I got Louis to okay this deal – which, I'd say, has about one snowball's chance in hell of happening - it would all be by the work of TWO good salespeople here: this "Clive", and Me. All you've done so far is to wet your pants.

JERRY: I'm going to be the big person here, Harry, and let that pass. It's still in my territory. No matter what. Even if it falls from the sky I get my half, okay?

HARRY (about to reply)

LOUIS (stands in the doorway to his office.) Harry! May I speak with you a moment?

       (JERRY still holds HARRY's attention.)

LOUIS: NOW.

HARRY: (to LOUIS) Sure.

JERRY: (patting HARRY on the shoulder) Get us this deal.

       (LOUIS ushers a limping HARRY into his office.)

LOUIS: What was that about?

HARRY: Oh, nothing.

LOUIS: Jerry was touching you.

HARRY: Just wishing me well, you know.

LOUIS: Yeah? Well. Come on in, Harry.
       (pacing, as HARRY slowly shuffles in)
How are you doing?

HARRY: Great! Couldn't be better. "Today is the best day of the year, no question!"

LOUIS: For God's sakes, Harry. Sit!

HARRY (collapses into the chair) Thanks.

LOUIS: So. How is that new fellow you recruited working out? Claude, isn't that his name?

HARRY: Yeah. Fine.

LOUIS: (nodding) A little green, maybe?

HARRY: He's got …an unusual style. Has made some good appointments! He's the son of an old war buddy of mine, you know.

LOUIS: No, didn't know.

> (Spot changes to CLAUDE's cubicle, where BOBBY is back leaning on CLAUDE.)

BOBBY: So. Shoot. How much you want?

CLAUDE: This is what I am trying to explain, Bobby. I mean, why am I talking to you?

BOBBY: You need a reason?

CLAUDE: Yeah, well, I could NOT talk to you.

BOBBY: Why you not want to talk? Oh, I get it. You are negotiating.

CLAUDE: You know, I think the reason I have trouble talking to you - and many people, for that matter - must be because I am in the weaker position here. And that, THAT is because… What is my motivation?
> (looks up)
I don't know what I want.

BOBBY: Good. So I tell you.

CLAUDE: I mean, I can't imagine what I would want, here, talking to you - besides shooting the breeze.

BOBBY: Good. So shooting the breeze is a good place to start.
Go ahead, shoot some breeze.

CLAUDE: (can't think of anything)

BOBBY: Good. Okay. So I take first shot.
      (a beat)
How you doin? Claude? Right?

CLAUDE: Right.

BOBBY: So where you from, Claude?

CLAUDE: Pretty much …here.

BOBBY: Not me. I from far away. But, find myself here, so make best of it, you know?

CLAUDE: (warming) I guess we can all relate in some manner or other to that, Bobby.

BOBBY: So how much you want to work for me?
      (a beat)
They say you pretty good. You pretty good? If you pretty good, we make a lot of money. I know. I leading salesman in area. You work for me, you work for the best. Harry, he "old lion", you know? A little tired. Losing his teeth, maybe? You make appointment for Harry, what happen? Maybe nothing. All that work lost. You get nothing. You work for me, nothing lost. You get say… one third. What you think about one third?

CLAUDE: (sighs) I suppose, Harry hired me. So I should work for Harry for a while.

BOBBY: Why wait?

CLAUDE: It's not my nature to move quickly.

BOBBY: This fast business. You got to move quickly.

CLAUDE: But I'm a slow person. I got to move slowly.

      (a beat)

BOBBY: You know what? You puzzle me. I wonder you any good, or not?
Maybe I not want to hire you. What you think of that?

CLAUDE: (starts to frame a reply)

BOBBY: (turns away to check calls on his cell.)

(Spotlight returns to LOUIS' office, downstage right.)

HARRY: You ever face down a bullet, Louis?

LOUIS: What kind of a question is that, Harry?

HARRY: A pretty simple question, Louis.

LOUIS: You mean, have I ever been mugged?

HARRY: No. I mean, have you ever been in an 'armed conflict'?

LOUIS: (laughs, nodding) Like where someone would be firing a bullet at me?

HARRY: Now we're making headway.

LOUIS: What are we getting at here, Harry? Because you know, I don't need to be told when I'm "making headway".

HARRY: C'mon, Louis. Just answer the question.

LOUIS: Alright. Because you're Harry, and because I like you Harry, I am going to answer that question.
          (a beat)
No.
          (before HARRY can respond)
Uh-uh! Now, before you ask another question I get to ask you one.
Who the hell is that bizarre kid you just hired? Because he doesn't look like a salesman to me. And I had an ironclad promise from you that if I let you stay on you would be hiring some real help... so that

you could stay on top of the most valuable territory in this district.

HARRY: Like I said, he's the son of a war buddy.

LOUIS: Oh, so that's what all this "facing down a bullet" stuff is about?

HARRY: The kid's good on the phones Louis. He's already made me lots of good appointments.

LOUIS: Which you can't get to Harry, because you're all crippled up!

HARRY: (stares at LOUIS)

LOUIS: I'm sorry. I didn't mean that the way it came out.

        (a beat)

HARRY: Louis. What is it you want to see me about?

LOUIS: You can't answer your e mails. Bobby says he can't even reach you by phone.

HARRY (scoffs) Bobby?

LOUIS: You can't meet your customers' demands. You can't even handle all of the appointments this new kid, whatevershisnameis, has made? Harry, what are you thinking?
        (a beat)
Let me tell you what you're thinking, because I don't think you even know. But I can tell you what you're thinking because I know YOU, Harry.
That kid's a ringer. You hired that kid, because you told me you would hire somebody. And then I took that on good faith and let you keep your job.

HARRY: "Let me keep my job?"

LOUIS: Is there an echo in here, or do you just like to hear me repeat myself? "I let you keep your job, because you hired that kid." WHO, I was led to believe, knew copier sales.

HARRY: He's worked with his wife, Mary Gustafson. You know her. She was the one who was giving us such fits in the 401 territory.

LOUIS: He's worked for his wife? So... Harry? Why didn't you hire his wife?

HARRY: She's busy.

LOUIS: How is she so busy, that she can have her husband working for us?

HARRY: She's pregnant.

LOUIS: Well good for her.

HARRY: They both seem pleased.

LOUIS: You know Harry. You can really irritate a person.
        (a beat)
What is this RESISTANCE I'm feeling? You hire the HUSBAND of a copier salesperson? Why not her uncle? Or maiden aunt? Or ...dog?
        (a beat)
You know why you never made manager, Harry?

HARRY: Louis. If you brought me in here to tell me why I never made manager, I think it's a little late in the game.

LOUIS: You know what I mean.

HARRY: (?)

LOUIS: Damn it Harry! You always have to be top dog. THAT's why you never made manager.

HARRY: Run that by me again?

LOUIS: You heard me. To be a manager Harry, you SOMETIMES have to give a little. I know, it's ironic, but you have to learn how to take advice, and to ADJUST.

HARRY: Alright Louis. Let me give you some advice.

LOUIS: Fuck you, Harry.

HARRY: You don't know squat about this kid I just hired. You just spoke with him for maybe five minutes, during which time you did all of the talking. Moreover, you don't listen worth a shit when you finally do shut your mouth. So don't tell me anything about my personnel, cause you. don't. know.
          (a beat)
And by the way...
               (HARRY raises a finger as if to impale LOIUS on a point,
               that he can't remember... all of a sudden.)

LOUIS: Harry.(snapping fingers) Harry!
               (waving his hand before HARRY's gaze)
Do you know where you are? Harry?

               (a long beat)

HARRY: (snapping back into awareness) In your office Louis.
               (taking a deep breath and collecting himself)
And I shouldn't have to tell you this.

LOUIS: You are sitting three feet from that door, Harry.
And do you know what is between you and that door, Harry?

HARRY: A lot of stuffy air?

LOUIS: I am, Harry. I am the ONLY one here, who is between you and that door.

HARRY: (grabbing for cane, rising unsteadily) And if you'd just get out of my way, I could leave.

LOUIS: You're not going anywhere. Sit down, Harry.

HARRY (pushing forward) Louis. I'm leaving.

LOUIS (pushing back, gently at first) No, Harry. You're staying.

>   (HARRY and LOUIS closer and closer into each other's
>   face.

HARRY: (raising voice, trying to shove around LOUIS)
I said, I'm LEAVING.

LOUIS" (blocking HARRY's exit) And I replied Harry,
        (into HARRY's ear, as if he were deaf)
NO HARRY. YOU'RE STAYING.

HARRY: (grappling) GET OUT OF MY WAY, LOUIS!

LOUIS: (grappling) SIT. DOWN! HARRY.

HARRY: (twisting LOUIS arm in an old army hold)   DON'T
MAKE ME HURT YOU, LOUIS.

>   (LOUIS grappling, and losing.)

LOUIS: YOU… OLD… FAHRT!

>   (LOUIS and HARRY struggle, with LOUIS finally shoving
>   HARRY back into his chair.)

>   (CLAUDE, meanwhile, has been watching and stands, not
>   knowing whether he should intercede.)

>   (LOUIS recovers. He glares at CLAUDE, then at
>   HARRY.)

LOUIS: You outta breath?

HARRY: (nods)

LOUIS: Yeah. I'm a little short of wind myself.
          (a beat)
Look Harry, this is not quite how I had intended this meeting to go.

HARRY: (waves him off) Don't spoil the moment.

LOUIS: (nods)
          (gestures that HARRY is free to leave)

          (HARRY eventually picks himself up and leaves LOUIS'
          office.)

SCENE 5

In music, as in everything, the disappearing moment of experience is the firmest reality."

- composer Benjamin Boretz

SETTING: Late that evening. The office is dark except for HARRY and CLAUDE's cubicle.

(HARRY and CLAUDE are drinking Jack Daniels out of Dixie cups. While HARRY is rummaging around in the scattered papers on his desk, he knocks his cane to the floor.)

CLAUDE: (handing HARRY his cane) Maybe we should call it a day, Harry.

HARRY: More e mails?

CLAUDE: Tom Skanzi. He keeps calling too.

HARRY: You want some investment advice?
          (a beat)
Stay married.

(THEY drink.)

CLAUDE: (smiling) You know Harry, Samuel Beckett was right: "Every word is like an unnecessary stain on the beauty of silence and nothingness."

HARRY: (grunts.)

CLAUDE: I used to work in a warehouse Harry, where let me tell you, the time passed slowly! It was like you waded through it on your way across those vast cement floors. And as my futility grew, I could see that life isn't just winning; there's a lot more to it. A lot more LOSING to it. And I began to see that the quick fun of winning begins to look more and more trivial against the somber deep grainy grays of loss... next to the monumental canyons of failure. And I became like an explorer! pushing through the undergrowth of enough drudgery, enough futility, of perhaps just one more day of this incredibly boring endeavor... until I had reached that secret place at the heart of it all, where it all becomes clear. Where activities and success arrange themselves into a perfect picture, like peaches and oranges in a Cezanne still life.
   (a beat)
Harry, it's all been done. It's all been said. It's just being traded back and forth, actually. You really haven't to do anything! As the Buddha says, "Don't just do something, stand there."

HARRY: (ignoring CLAUDE)
...The worse we look on that board, the harder it's going to get. They're going to be clamoring for Louis to take my territory. It'll be the Bobbies, and the very aggressive youngsters who'll come after us first. Bobby will probably even cast the idea around the office... just to make us look soft, and to piss me off. Donovan is such a candy-ass, he'd probably go for it. And Louis will listen, just to show his mind is open But he's too savvy to cede them a major territory like this.
We don't have to worry much about the more senior, established salespeople. They're not going to want to pull up stakes when they're already doing well.
No, our worry from that quarter is that they are going to start stealing our best technicians, and pushing to the front of the line for boxes. And it's going to start getting hard to deliver on the deals we've already signed. And we're going to be busier and busier putting out brush fires as the service support is drawn away and given to others who are beating their quota. So all of these other factors are already in play, even as we sit here.

(to CLAUDE) I want you to understand how the energy is flowing out all the time. So that you'll understand how important it is to put on your game face!

CLAUDE: (sits up)

HARRY: (frowns) And to work like hell! ... while we're here.
No. Louis is going to go out and try to lure some big hitter away from the competition. He'll guarantee him at least a hundred grand for the first year.
          (a beat)
That's why Louis lost his composure, today. He'd probably just returned from a luncheon, already schmoozing my replacement. And he feels bad about it. Or maybe, at least, uneasy. Louis is waiting for us to fail.

CLAUDE: (nodding) So I think that there are two ways of gauging reality, Harry.
          (HARRY stares at CLAUDE.)
One is by changing it. The second is by suffering it.
          (CLAUDE's finger waves back and forth between them.)
And I believe the mind is constantly toggling between these two poles in an effort to make sense of things. So, you know, I think that if I could design the perfect thing to be... I would be a has-been. Maybe because, I don't see your situation as deterioration, Harry. I see it as a wonderful freedom, and also just the wonder of lying back and seeing what happens.
It's like looking up at the stars.
          (sighs, and he leans back with his Dixie cup of drink)
I know I enjoy Kevin Costner in all his has-been roles.

HARRY: Kevin Costner, huh?

CLAUDE: (nods) Most has-beens aren't really fitted for the role. They are still too anchored in the past. Too hostile to their fate. And usually in the movies they have to make a come-back. But the ones I enjoy are where they've already been somebody, and then they move on from that. This is something Kevin Costner is particularly good at portraying, I feel.

HARRY: Claude. I ever tell you about Bill?

CLAUDE: ?

HARRY: Bill …Gustafson. Your father!
     (a beat)
He was a private in my company, you know. In his own way - just like you - he was FASCINATING, because… No matter what he said, no one could listen.
     (a beat)
He would shout, "Incoming!" And no one would listen. Apparently we all had to see the shells hit first. Go figure.
Anyway. We'd be getting up for going out on patrol and I'd shout to Bill, "How you feeling today, Bill?" You know, trying to get him to say something.
     "I've felt better," he'd say.
So, we'd go out on patrol. And after we'd fired off a few rounds, I'd turn to him, and all he'd have to say was, "Can we go now?"
Anyway, one afternoon, we came into a big firefight, and … this mortar struck us. Really messed me up. And when I woke, I was too weak to move, and deafened by the concussion. But there was Bill, pretty as you please. I swear, not even a hair mussed.
     "Can we go now?" I remember Bills lips moving.
     "Yes! Bill", I said. "We can go now!"
     (a beat)
I was in the infirmary for six months following that one. One day soon after, the CO came to see me. He shook my hand and said:
     "Well now I know why the Bill Gustafson's of this world are put here. It's to save Harry Coombs' sorry ass."
     (upbeat)
You know, Claude. That MUST be why you're here.
I have no idea how you Gustafsons are going to do it, this time. But let me tell you, I'm all ears.
     (pulls out a thick fold of money with good hand)
     (counts out bills)
I want you here Monday in a full suit, and looking like a top of the line salesman. Here's nine hundred dollars for the transformation.
Just ask your wife to outfit you. Sounds like she knows the business.

(a beat)

But… before you buy anything, I want you to shop and to compare and to find out everything you can about that suit of clothes. Then I want you to find out everything you can about that pair of shoes. Then I want you to find out everything you can about that pair of socks, tie, belt and shirt. Then I want you to find out everything you can about your hair jell. Then I want you to find out everything you can about your toothpaste, your underarm deodorant, the razorblades, your barber and haberdasher… need I go on?

(CLAUDE sighs.)

Being a salesman is a lot like being an actor, Claude. Only instead of playing a character, you're playing… stuff.

Be here Monday morning, 7:30 am sharp, and we'll talk.

(HARRY puts his hand on CLAUDE's shoulder as they rise to leave.)

We're going to make a REAL 'has-been' of you yet!

(lights out)

END OF ACT ONE

ACT TWO

SCENE 1

SETTING: That next Monday morning, spotlight is on CLAUDE downstage right, preparing himself in an (imaginary) bathroom mirror for work.

AT RISE: CLAUDE is admiring himself in his bathroom mirror.

CLAUDE: I am this EXPENSIVE shirt…I am a nice tie. (straightening tie) I am a POWER tie. (checking himself) I am: Hair gel. Shave. Cologne. Whitened teeth. (dusts jacket) …Coat. (turns in the mirror) I'm a SUIT. I'm a SEVEN HUNDRED DOLLAR! suit. And great shoes. Cashmere socks! (patting pockets, as if gun holsters) Cell phone… Palm pilot…

> (CLAUDE turns, walks upstage.)

> (7:30 am sharp, at the cubicle. HARRY is
> already there, as CLAUDE enters.)

HARRY: Good. You're here.

CLAUDE: Off the rack and ready to roll.

HARRY : Not yet. Where'd you get those shoes? I like those.

CLAUDE: McSweeney's.

HARRY: What kind are they?

CLAUDE: (shrugs) Your standard brown dress shoe.

HARRY: Standard? Brown?

CLAUDE: Actually... they're not standard. They're English imports with a special business persons' insole and cushioned heels for busy people who are on their feet a lot. And the color is actually called... Portuguese Cork! AND if you'll notice the lighter, ventilated Spanish vamp? They're cooler. Still in style but knocked down to thirty percent off when I purchased them with the cashmere socks.

HARRY: Nice.

CLAUDE: Calf-height, with special ribbed top to prevent crawl.

HARRY: Like I said, nice. I see you went with suspenders. I've been thinking of doing that myself.

CLAUDE: They allow for a little more flair, look good with pleated slacks, and they don't form a lip for your gut to hangover.

HARRY: You don't have a gut.

CLAUDE: And I don't aim to get one, Harry. We stay lean, and mean, is what I say.

HARRY: Nice shirt. What's the thread count?

    (a beat)

CLAUDE: I don't know, Harry.

HARRY: You know the thread count is one measure of the fineness of a fabric.

CLAUDE: I'd only run into that in bed sheets.

HARRY: Basically, it's true for any fabric. Some of the Italian silks, the ties, especially, have thread counts into the triple digits.

CLAUDE: Thank you. That's handy to know.

HARRY: Good! You've stroked me a little. And shown that you can listen. So take a turn.
          (CLAUDE turns rapidly.)
But don't do what I ask so quickly. You're rolling over like a dog. Say something to advertise that you are making a concession. Offering an accommodation. Okay. So now, turn.

CLAUDE: (considers) Sure.

HARRY: Who's your tailor?

CLAUDE: Juan Gomez.

HARRY: Who?

CLAUDE: Would you like his card?

HARRY: (shrugs) Can't hurt.

CLAUDE: Would you hold this for me a moment?

          (offering HARRY his coat)

HARRY: That's right! Dominate the situation as quickly as possible.

          (THEY exchange overcoat and card.)

CLAUDE: Here you go.

HARRY: Excellent. We've just done business.

CLAUDE: I wrote my name and number on the back. In case there's any problem, just have Juan call me.

HARRY: And we're associates. (palms card) I believe I might be hatching a terror.
     (a beat)
So, I guess we take it to the next level.

CLAUDE: ? (as HARRY circles)

HARRY: From our time together I have gathered that poetry is not just words, any more than the label on a wine bottle is the wine. Have I remembered that comparison fairly?

CLAUDE: Yes. I believe so…

HARRY: (interrupting) POETRY is about "authenticity", "the song and dance of the soul!" … and "being true to yourself". We empathize and in turn are empathized with, and boundaries dissolve as our 'dormant' inner creative selves begin to 'breath' and to swell! … until our needs, and the audience's, meet - in something quite beyond words - in a wonderful synergistic spasm of mutual and universal regard. It sounds like pretty fair sex, actually!
Have I got that about right?

CLAUDE: Well, I suppose so.

HARRY: Business is different. Business is about STUFF. Who's got it. And who wants it.
     (a beat)
So. Are you ready? Here we go:
My former brother-in-law Don, had a suit like that.

CLAUDE: (nods)

HARRY: It fell apart on him.
            (stepping forward, very aggressively)
When he first came over, dressed like that, (laughs) we couldn't
believe our eyes.
            (HARRY touches CLAUDE's lapel.)
But here, let me tell you a little more about Don.
            (HARRY grips lapel as CLAUDE steps back.)
I mean, this guy, well, he can be real entertaining. You'll like his
story. I laugh louder each time I tell it.
            (CLAUDE retreats.)
You want to hear more about this, or not?
            (HARRY tosses up his hands.)
WHERE ARE YOU GOING?

CLAUDE: Just allowing myself a comfortable distance, Harry.

HARRY: Get back in here.

CLAUDE: (moves forward a half-step)

HARRY: No. I mean right up here. I want you in my face!

            (HARRY keeps motioning, and CLAUDE keeps moving
            until he's in HARRY's face.)

CLAUDE: (having trouble speaking so closely) It's just that when
you come on so strong, I can't think.

HARRY: (leaning in) People come on strong! That's sales. That's
life!

CLAUDE: Maybe if …you just didn't get so upset?

HARRY: You want the customer's money?   They're going to get
upset!

CLAUDE: Okay…

HARRY: You've got MY money? I'M going to get upset!!

CLAUDE: Well... alright.

HARRY : (bearing in) So you're going to have to fight. You're going to have to YELL!

CLAUDE: Well... OKAY!!!

HARRY: So quit clinging to this nervous little construction that calls itself Claude, and join in. Don't be buffaloed. Most of this world is just one big pussy! all lathered up and waiting. And it's out there getting all impatient! It WANTS for you to GRAB it.

CLAUDE: But I'm best on the phone. Really Harry, I can grab best over the phone.

HARRY: (wheeling around) No. You can't do this over the phone. I've just suffered a stroke! You think that if I were able to run around like a Spring Chicken, I would be HERE, instead of out THERE, grabbing for it myself?
    (poking CLAUDE in the chest)
You're telling people they're a LITTLE mistaken. Because you want their money!
    (poking CLAUDE)
So of course! they're going to be a LITTLE leery. So, of course!, things may a LITTLE... volatile. So, you may yell.... THEY may yell... But it's just a game, you see?
    (HARRY grabs CLAUDE's index finger and pokes himself
    with it.)
You see? (pokes) Fuck me.

    (CLAUDE begins to poke HARRY, as if testing rising
    dough.)

HARRY: You feel yourself beginning to smile? That's right.
    (HARRY pokes CLAUDE)
 And fuck you back! Because it's me, mirroring YOUR energy and handing it back.
    (as they poke each other)

Fuck you. And fuck me.
"I'm okay." And, "You're okay." You see?

CLAUDE: (catching on) And fuck you too!

HARRY: And, fuck you first.

CLAUDE: And FUCK YOU! second. And fuck you! third…
        (wheeling in a circle, pointing at the other cubicles)
and forth, and fifth, and sixth!

HARRY: (mystified)

CLAUDE: Sorry.
        (lowering his finger and putting it away)
But I guess then, (smiling) that I CAN think of a few things to say!

HARRY: Great! Then there you are. And here WE go.
        (Clapping CLAUDE hard on the back.)
You see, this is what sales teaches us again and again. It is clinging to
our failures which depletes us. It is clinging to those all-too-habitual
destructive behaviors. When what we all need to do is to grasp for
that first nebulous air of success. That first little tingle, marking the
engorgement of Mister Richard. (smiles) Don't be so afraid to go
out there and have social intercourse. Don't be afraid to mate. You
just have to let the little monster out, my boy!

CLAUDE: Okay!

HARRY: Don't ever be afraid Claude, to toss out those brand new
shoes and to buy even NEWER ones. Because YOU are READY,
Claude, to be something NEW! or even NEWER!! Because
"attention must to be paid."
So,
    "My former brother-in-law Don, had a suit like that."

CLAUDE: (nods) And I'll bet you bought it for him!

        (a beat)

HARRY: Now you've pissed me off!

CLAUDE: Gee... sorry.

HARRY: You're not here to piss me off! You're here to defend the Value of Your Suit. So that I will take IT, and therefore YOU, seriously.

CLAUDE: Okay, Harry.
But do you really think that the value of my suit matters one dust mote in the grand scheme of things? Because what is there about all this that feeds our sense of WONDER, Harry? About ourselves? About me? About you! (poking) About who we are? About *Where Do We Come From? What Are We? Where Are We Going? (Gauguin)*

HARRY: Why can't you just bring yourself to say, "Harry, I have a newborn son. (poking) I need a job! Because MONEY is what I really need?"

CLAUDE: Well, yeah. There's that.

HARRY: Is this 'thing' you call Claude - and clutch so tightly - really your creation? Or is it the leftovers? The stinky, rotten, picked-over pieces the stronger personalities out there have discarded? Take a look around. Where's that part of you which says, "Hey! These guys are assholes, and I'm taking back what's mine!" Why don't you try WINNING for a change, and THEN decide "what you really want?'
      (a beat)
Don't you understand?! That no matter WHO you are; no matter WHAT you've got! Or THINK you've got... They're going to try and take it away from you?!

CLAUDE: You're starting to sound a little rebellious yourself here, Harry.

HARRY: You're damned right!
So... "My brother-in-law, Don, had a suit just like that. And it fell apart on him!"

What do you say?!

      (pacing back and forth like a drill sergeant)

This is not parlor conversation I'm teaching you. This is a Basic Conversation 101. I say something to you; and then you say something back to me, that lands just where I left the conversation with you. It doesn't have to go off into the stars. It doesn't have to ask itself whether we are "actually having a 'relationship'" ? …And it doesn't have to impress me with its BRILLIANCE. It stays put! …on the same yard line where the tackle was made. It's pretty mundane. You got me, soldier?

CLAUDE: (straightens) Yes, …sir?

HARRY: "My brother-in-law, Don, had a suit just like that. And it fell apart on him!" What do you say?

CLAUDE: "It couldn't be like this suit."

HARRY: (eyeing CLAUDE) What a sad sack. What did you say?!

CLAUDE: (standing at stiff attention) "It could NOT be like this suit, sir!"

HARRY: (staring him down like a drill sergeant) And WHY IS THAT?

      (BOBBY, passing by, overhears.)

CLAUDE: "BECAUSE THIS IS A FINE SUIT, SIR!"

BOBBY: So. How things going?

HARRY: (starting to stride back and forth) WHAT DID YOU SAY, SALESMAN?!

BOBBY: (brightening) Pretty good, I think. Yes?

HARRY & CLAUDE: (to BOBBY) Piss off!

BOBBY: (scurrying off) Pretty good, I think.

CLAUDE: Because this suit will NOT fall apart? BECAUSE THIS SUIT IS MADE TO WEAR LIKE IRON.
   (HARRY nods.)
Go ahead! Pull on this sleeve! Feel the fabric!
   (HARRY pulls on the sleeve.)
It will wear like iron, but it FEELS like silk...?

HARRY: That's better. Much better.
   (a beat)
At ease.

CLAUDE: (sighs, collapses into relaxed posture)

   (HARRY takes out binders, pamphlets, brochures to create
   a great pile of informational material.)

HARRY: Our customers are not necessarily friendly people, Claude. They are people with NEEDS. The very ESSENCE of Sales is to "play the ball where it lies". This might sound easy, but it's not. In fact, it's the hardest thing in the world. In fact – and this might be of interest to someone with your turn of mind, Claude – it's the hardest thing in life to do.
Attention!

CLAUDE: "Sir!"

HARRY: Next assignment!
   (HARRY hands this great pile of information to CLAUDE.)
We're ready to talk about the stuff which makes us money.

SCENE 2

SETTING: Same. HARRY has left. CLAUDE is role-playing.

CLAUDE (A): (passing brochure from left hand to the right)
The BizHub 1050. With a 105 page per minute production speed, it's an incredible addition to the hi-end market.

CLAUDE (B): (right hand looking it over)
Why would we need a 105 page per minute copier?

CLAUDE (A): Because your time is precious? Because you can get there 105 pages per minute faster?

CLAUDE (B): (handing material back)
If we have that big of a job we send it out.

CLAUDE (A): (handing it back)
Why not keep it in house, and have your equipment make you money?

CLAUDE (B): (handing it back)
I'd have to hire a whole new employee to run it.

CLAUDE (A): (handing it back)
You certainly do enough to make it worth your while.

CLAUDE (B:) (handing it back)
I don't want something this large clogging up our already crammed office!

CLAUDE (A): ?

CLAUDE (B): Your machine is too big!

CLAUDE (A): Your office is too small!

CLAUDE (B): Now you're being silly.

CLAUDE (A): No, really!
     (a beat, as CLAUDE hands the brochure to the other hand)
Our machine has been "sized-efficient".

CLAUDE (B): (tossing brochure to the floor)
What the hell does that mean?

     (a beat, as CLAUDE recovers brochure)

CLAUDE (A): I'm glad you asked!

BOBBY: (enters) So. Sound like you and Harry get into it big time, huh?

CLAUDE: (remembering to 'poke' back)
Why do you always think we're fighting? We're practicing selling. You know, sales?

BOBBY: Well, it sound like fight.

CLAUDE: A lot of sales sound like fight.

BOBBY: (giggles) That's true!
     (BOBBY's cell phone rings.)
Excuse me.
     (answers phone)
Yeah. Oh hi! I meaning to call you! Just thinking right now, got to call Anita.
     (a long beat)
They said it would do that. Honest. It's what they all say to me. In fact, they all say this is what is extra special about this machine, that it do that. So, I figure it must do that. I mean, these are all very technologically savvy people, you know?
     (a beat)
But he tell me it does do that.
     (a beat)
But why would I say it doesn't do that, if he tell me it does?
     (a long beat)
I know. I know. Is bad. But I think I know way out.

(a beat)

Yeah. Yeah. I know I said that, but listen. Here is even better deal, I think.

(a beat)

Yeah. Yeah. I know. I know. But you haven't heard better deal.

(BOBBY looks around so as to move out of earshot.)

Okay. Here it is. Here is better deal.

(BOBBY leaves stage.)

SCENE 3

SETTING: Same. Morning, several days later. CLAUDE is wearing his snazzy new suit, carrying a new briefcase he has been loading with brochures…, and his hair is moussed.

HARRY: So. You know what to do?

CLAUDE: Just be myself, right?

HARRY: No!
       (a beat)
Basically, any problem they have - you can make go away.
Whenever you see a lemon, your job is to make lemonade.
So, confidence! Got that?

CLAUDE: I'm telling you Harry, as soon as people meet me things go downhill…

HARRY: Then you'll have to start closing as soon as you can.

CLAUDE: It feels all wrong.
       (HARRY frowns)
But then, on the other hand - the way I am - I could suffer an epiphany in the coming moments, and from this newer perspective it could appear just the thing to do!

HARRY: There you go. That's the spirit! A salesman always leans towards the bright side. Just like a plant.

CLAUDE: This is going to require a lot of optimism. But I like the plant metaphor. I believe I'm naturally phototropic.

HARRY: That's right, you're heading towards the light.

CLAUDE: It's dark all around - in the earth, ON this earth! - and yet, I feel myself being "drawn towards the light".

HARRY: That's right, actually. And the trick is, to hear those voices calling to you.

CLAUDE: (getting into it) …to leave my body. To "shuffle off this mortal coil"!

HARRY: No! To close the deal! To experience a little success!
        (a beat)
For Pete's sakes, Claude. People are looking all over for a WINNER. They are virtually scouring the landscape to find a winner. They are searching for YOUR success because they want to become associated with success THEMSELVES. And indeed, I am offering YOU this success, because I would like some MYSELF!
        (a beat)
So can you feel the nearness of the opportunity I'm offering you? In fact, this whole world is offering you?

CLAUDE: I think so. Maybe.

HARRY: (offers his hand) You just have to reach out and grasp it.

CLAUDE: Okay.

HARRY: But you have to be sure.

CLAUDE: I think I'm sure.

HARRY: You have to be sure you're sure.

CLAUDE: I believe I'm sure!

HARRY: But you have to be SURE you're SURE!

CLAUDE: (drinks the Kool Aid) For SURE, I'm sure!

HARRY: (grasping CLAUDE's hand with both of his)
He's SURE, he's SURE!

(BOTH stand there for a moment in blissful communion.)

HARRY: (shoving him out the door) Go. Go!...

SCENE 4

SETTING: Same. CLAUDE returns disheveled from the field.

CLAUDE: (drops file folder after file folder onto HARRY's desk)
No show. No money. No credit.
      (offering HARRY another file)
They said, they liked me a lot.

HARRY: (setting it with the others on the pile) Generally a bad
sign.

CLAUDE: (nodding, setting another) They said it wasn't ME; it was
them. (waving another) They said it wasn't them; it was ME.

HARRY: (laughs.)

CLAUDE: (waves last failed proposal) AND, his brother in law
works for Ikon.

HARRY: Well… (smiles, as he takes it) Does he like his brother in
law?

CLAUDE: (frowns)

LOUIS: (on phone to DEAN in his office) HARRY.

(LOUIS motions HARRY into his office.)
(HARRY rises and walks into LOUIS' office.)
(CLAUDE goes through some more of the stack by himself
at his own desk.)

CLAUDE: Happy with the current vendor. UNhappy with US. No
money in budget. Liked the Canon better. …just purchased!

    (CLAUDE begins to pound his head loudly on the stack of
    failed proposals.)

    (LOUIS is talking with DEAN on the phone, while
    HARRY waits. They will conduct their meeting to the
    loud sound of CLAUDE beating his head on the
    desk… like a metronome.)

    (DEAN's tirade is recorded so that when LOUIS holds the
    phone from his ear, it is played VERY loudly over the
    house speakers.)

DEAN's VOICE: He hired the HUSBAND of a copier salesperson?
WHY NOT HER MAIDEN AUNT? OR NEIGHBOR? OR….
DOG?

    (LOUIS jerks the phone from his ear, holding it out.)

LOUIS: (nodding to HARRY) We covered that.
(listening) Okay. Okay.

    (holding phone away)

DEAN's VOICE: You tell that sorry Son of a Bitch, Harry, that he
better have found himself one hellofa poet… 'Cause I don't give a
rat's ass…
    (a beat)
And by the way, Louis. You and I need to have a talk.

    (LOUIS listens some more, then hangs up, as if barely

closing the gate on a dog.)

HARRY: You look stressed, Louis.

LOUIS: This is not stress, Harry. This is CONCERN. What I have is a 'look of CONCERN'.

HARRY: (nodding) You look 'concerned', Louis.

(LOUIS looks out at the board, which doesn't look good especially for HARRY, and then at CLAUDE, who is pounding his head on his desk.)

LOUIS: I AM concerned.

(HARRY follows LOUIS gaze.)

(BOTH watch CLAUDE banging his head on his desk.)

HARRY: Pretty soon he will realize that it works better if he uses his head to hammer on the customer, rather than his desk … and things will be fine.

LOUIS: …"things will be fine". Harry. You know what I would really like?

HARRY: No, Louis. What would you really like?

LOUIS: What I would really like Harry, is for you to retire - at the peak of your game.

HARRY: What I think Louis, is that what you'd "really like" is for me to 'retire'.

LOUIS: Well. Isn't that what we'd all like Harry? I mean, you just heard all that craziness, right?

HARRY: I don't know, Louis. Maybe YOU should retire. After all, you're looking stressed. You're sounding stressed. And, by the way,

(waving at the board)
...your numbers aren't looking all that good.

LOUIS: Harry. If I have a look, that 'look' is concern.

HARRY: Okay, Louis, fine. You have a very, 'concerned', look. So... Maybe you should retire?

LOUIS: You know Harry. I bring you in here. I try to talk to you. And what I get, is this RESISTANCE.

HARRY: What you're seeing Louis is determination. This is my look of 'determination'. You seem to see a look of determination as resistance, Louis. You should look into that. I think you have a blind side. You should be happy. You have a very DETERMINED employee.

LOUIS: Well, you LOOK tired.

HARRY: (waving to indicate CLAUDE) Actually, TWO, very 'determined' employees.

(BOTH look at CLAUDE with his head collapsed on his desk.)

LOUIS: Frankly, you BOTH look tired.

(lights out)

SCENE 5

SETTING: Office. CLAUDE is in full lotus position with bandaged forehead and quietly meditating, when LOUIS appears. At first LOUIS looks like he may fly into a rage, but collects himself.

LOUIS: (smiling) What are you doing?

CLAUDE: (waving) Oh, hi Louis.

LOUIS: (waving broadly) Hi!
        (a beat)
What are you doing?

CLAUDE: Recharging my batteries. Cleaning up the mental energies, you know.

LOUIS: ?

CLAUDE: (in confidence) I'm trying to reach Level 3.

LOUIS: Level 3? What is that, a new start-up?

CLAUDE: No. It's the Final Level of Harry's Training Program.

LOUIS: (nodding) "The Final Level of Harry's Training Program."

CLAUDE: Yes. It's dark on this earth, and all around, and yet the trick is to hear those voices calling to you.

LOUIS: "...voices calling to you."

CLAUDE: Harry says they're there. You just have to listen.

LOUIS: Harry says this?

CLAUDE: Harry says this.

LOUIS: You know Harry's recently suffered a stroke.

CLAUDE: Yeah.

LOUIS: Yeah. So what do these "voices" say to you?

CLAUDE: Harry says they are saying, "Yes." They are telling me that they want to be associated with me, that they want me to be successful; because they want to be associated with success.

LOUIS: Harry says they are saying all this?

CLAUDE: (nods)

LOUIS: So is this what you are hearing? When you are doing this? You're hearing a lot of voices saying, "Yes!"

CLAUDE: Well, no. Not yet anyway. But I'm listening! Harry says the trick is to go for the light. To focus on that one little ray of light where the voices are saying, "Yes!" and to go for that.

LOUIS: But you don't hear anything?

CLAUDE: In all honesty?

(LOUIS nods gravely.)

CLAUDE: No.

LOUIS: Well you know what? You're in luck. Because I'm a voice calling to you. And I have something to say.

CLAUDE: What's that?

LOUIS: My idea is that maybe you can't hear these voices - because they're too. Far. AWAY.

CLAUDE: ?

LOUIS: (leaning in like a drill sergeant) You want to hear, "Yes"?
        (CLAUDE nods.)
You want to hear it really LOUD?
        (CLAUDE nods, hesitantly.)
Then GO, and get into the CUSTOMER'S FACE!

        (CLAUDE nods rapidly, then grabs his things and scurries off.)

SCENE 6

SETTING: The office, days later. CLAUDE has finally closed a sale or two. HARRY doesn't look great on the board, but they're on the board.

BOBBIE: (indicating board) Hey! You looking a little-bitty better. I hear you get into Old Stone Bank! Nobody from here ever get into Old Stone. Except maybe to rob it, you know?

CLAUDE: (so used to mirroring the customer, he starts mimicking BOBBY) Hey! You smart? Maybe you work for me?

BOBBIE: Ha, ha! Maybe good idea! I tell you, this month is tough. Got to make one hundred thousand dollars.
    (checking cellular)
Where I going to make one hundred thousand dollars? You got any ideas?
    (no phone messages, shuts phone)
I think maybe you got some ideas. I mean, you working for Harry, you know?

CLAUDE: Harry says, "Claude. Play ball where it lies."

BOBBY: Harry says that?

CLAUDE: Harry says that.

BOBBY: And that work for you?

CLAUDE: So far, so good ...and getting better! you know?

(BOBBY looks at the board.)

BOBBY: What that mean? Where is ball lying?
     (a beat)
I mean, maybe you tell me where ball is, then?

CLAUDE: Ball is like, the way things are, you know? So, it means, you look at how things are – then you sell there.

BOBBY: Sounds good! I think. I mean, the "selling", you know. So how are things? I mean, which "way" are things?

CLAUDE: I'm glad you asked! Because things going good for me, you know? Things going REAL good. And you want to know why? I tell you why. (confidentially) I never ask customer to buy.

BOBBY: You never ask customer to buy? How you sell anything?

CLAUDE: They ask me to sell! And then, you see, that's where the ball is.

BOBBY: Yeah. I think. You say, Harry tell you this?

CLAUDE: One of Harry's most closest kept secrets.

BOBBY: No kidding?

CLAUDE: No kidding.

BOBBY: You know, I like you. You remind me of someone.

CLAUDE: You meet all sort in Sales!

BOBBY: That for sure, brother.

    (CLAUDE and BOBBY slap hands.)

    (BOBBY's cell rings.)

BOBBY: Oh! Excuse me, please.

     (BOBBY wanders off to take his call.)

     (CLAUDE returns to his paperwork.)

     (CLAUDE's phone rings.)

CLAUDE: Claude Gustafson.
     (listens)
Oh hi. Jared! So glad you call. I was just thinking, got to call Jared.
     (listens)
Well, because... there's new wrinkle, you know? Yeah. BETWEEN
now and then. Yeah, that I thought we ought discuss. You know,
meet again? Talk, a little? ...more.
     (listens)
Yeah. Well, that just makes it more important we talk, you know?
     (shaking head)
Okay, fine. But here is wrinkle!
     (listens)
You want to hear wrinkle?
     (listens)
Yeah, this Claude. (laughs) Who you think I am?
     (listens)
Some Russian/ Near Eastern gangster?
     (a long beat, as CLAUDE pauses to focus.)
     (CLAUDE makes loud sound of clearing sinuses.)
Sorry, Jared. It must have been my sinuses!
     (listens)
Yeah. You know the workplace... You can catch anything... But
listen. There's something here that's come up, that I think we ought
to talk about.

SCENE 7

SETTING: The next day in LOUIS' office.

LOUIS: You know, I'm not going to sit here Harry, and tell you that this isn't a young person's game.

HARRY: (friendly) I didn't anticipate that you would, Louis.

LOUIS: (leaning forward to get HARRY's attention.) You know what the irony of our situation is Harry?
    (a beat)
If you hadn't been such a great salesperson – but say someone of the caliber of a Jerry or Bobby - we could have afforded to deadwood you until the last tooth fell from that stubborn, contentious smile of yours!
However, this division has grown to rely upon you for over 40 percent of its revenue. We cannot afford to lose 40 percent of our revenue.

HARRY: We're working the problem, Louis. The kid is starting to get his bearings. I can feel it.

LOUIS: You can feel it.

HARRY: (nods) I can feel it.

LOUIS: (glancing at the board) Harry. The numbers don't lie.

HARRY: Yes, Louis. But there's kind of a limited number of things they can discuss – don't you think?

(a beat)

LOUIS: Harry, I just walked out there and found him in FULL LOTUS POSITION …in MY BULLPEN! And do you know what he said?

HARRY: (sighs) What did he say?

LOUIS: (imitating CLAUDE's wave)
He said, "Oh, hi! Louis."

HARRY: (nodding) …nice kid.

LOUIS: …"nice kid"? Let's cut to the chase here Harry. Dean says, and I quote: "YOU CUT THAT KID LOOSE!" - and we can start over fresh. We install someone of OUR OWN choosing to HELP you in your territory – while you are getting over this rough spot – and we can go from there.

HARRY: …"and we can go from there." A deal is a deal, Louis.

LOUIS: No it isn't Harry. That's what you have never been able to grasp. A deal, is whatever Dean SAYS it is.

HARRY: You know that's not square.

LOUIS: "Square"? "Square" is whatever Dean says it is. And I have to say, that I tend to side with Dean here on that. You haven't been "square" with US, here, Harry.
You and I both know that I had an ironclad promise from you that if I let you stay on you would be hiring some real help.
(a beat)
For Godsakes, Harry? What is it about this KID that you find so appealing?

HARRY: I trust him.

(a long beat)

LOUIS: (aggrieved) Harry? Why don't you trust me? Why don't you trust Dean? I know, for a fact, that you wouldn't have worked for this company all these years, if it wasn't run straight.

HARRY: Okay, Louis. Let's imagine that you're a sharp guy.

(LOUIS stares hard at HARRY)

LOUIS: Where are we going with this Harry?

HARRY: And you have a long-time employee. The guy's at the top of his trade, and he's been making you a LOT of money for a LOT of years. But! the guy's getting older. And you know one of these days he's going to have to quit.

LOUIS: Just what I've been saying, all along, Harry. Everybody, sooner or later, has to retire. The old has to make way for the new.

HARRY: (nodding) And you're wondering of course, how you are going to get RID of him – put in a younger guy with more energy who stands to increase the revenue - without losing the older guys contacts and his accounts?

LOUIS: Harry, you're trying to make me look like the bad guy here.

HARRY: And it would be nice if it could happen… that is, if you didn't have to wait until the last tooth fell from this guy's "contentious smile" - you know?
Because you're sharp enough to know that this guy has some very big accounts which are very loyal to him, personally.

LOUIS: Exactly what I've been saying, Harry. Some of these guys would walk across cut glass to do business with YOU!

HARRY: (nods) You may even be getting some heat about it from the man upstairs.

LOUIS: (nodding, with finger tips together in prayer position) That wouldn't surprise me at all.

HARRY: So you figure, why not hire a young man — some young TURK - who this old FART can mentor and train, and then eventually grab his slot? And, lo and behold! your prayers are answered. And instead of having to watch your revenues fall while "waiting for that last tooth..." ...He suffers a stroke. And you say to him, "Harry! I will let you keep your job, if you will hire someone to help you over the rough spots."

LOUIS: Harry, you know, when you're not doing well, everyone can look like your enemy.

HARRY: Right. So Harry does the 'right' thing and hires someone to assist him, until he gets back on his feet.

LOUIS: Yeah, but he hires a POET, for Pete's sake.

HARRY: That's kind of funny, isn't it, Louis? 'Poetic Justice'

(LOUIS laughs lightly, while shaking his head.)

LOUIS: Damn it, Harry. I'm really going to miss you.

HARRY: (rising to leave) Not until I'm gone, Louis. Not until I'm gone.

LOUIS: (calling after) Oh, you're gone alright!

SCENE 8

SETTING: Later. Their numbers are looking better. And CLAUDE is at his desk, working.

CLAUDE: (on phone) That's right Dan. Sure we have eCopy. ("Ee-Copy")

> (JERRY enters, and waits impatiently to speak with CLAUDE.)

CLAUDE: (on phone) Reassure Wendy that Konica Minolta has the easiest user interface on the market.
> (listens)

Trust me, in a week she'll be doing everything she's doing now on those beaters, and you'll be saving yourself around FOUR THOUSAND dollars.
> (listens)

Yes. And this will be with all new equipment.
> (listens)

That's right! The buyout is calculated in.
> (listens)

Fine. But I'm giving up a few points on this to make it all happen already. Because we're in a squeeze here. And the boss will go for this deal a lot quicker if we wrap it by the end of the month. Well, yeah, I mean Harry.

Good as can be expected, I think
> (listens)

We could do that. Sure.

No problem.

Sure.

      (listens)
No. Can't do that.
      (listens)
If I did that Dan, Harry would kick my ass from hell to breakfast.
      (listens)
Yeah, he could still do it!
      (listens)
Okay, fine then. I'll bring the paper work by tomorrow.
      (a beat)
Good talking to you too, Dan.
      (hangs up)

JERRY: Harry talk to Louis yet?

CLAUDE: About what?

JERRY: About the Owens account!

CLAUDE: Owens Blister-packaging, the start-up?

JERRY: Yeah. He mention it?

CLAUDE: That's the one in your territory who you're tight with the owner in?

JERRY: We have some rapport, I think. Why? What has Harry been saying?

CLAUDE: Harry's been kind of mum.

JERRY: Mum? What does "mum" mean?
Maybe you should make this plain to Harry. The end of ANOTHER month is upon us. We put the nail in this thing right away, and by that I mean immediately! or there's no deal. Clive is calling me nearly once a day. This is a 'VANISHING' opportunity. The guy needs the equipment, and he needs it now. Otherwise we lose him to a cost per copy service. I've got signed leases. All I need is Louie's approval with the leasing companies.

CLAUDE: (rising) Walk with me Jerry.

JERRY: (looking around) Walk with you?

CLAUDE: (moving) You're imagining this in terms of money.

JERRY: Bingo!

> (JERRY falls in as they pace back and forth – out of 'earshot'.)

CLAUDE: That's not the way to think of it. Just let me continue. We imagine this from the point of view of the leasing company, and it's not about money... Just let me continue. It's about risk. So you see, if we roll this problem around from the leasing company's point of view, the money problem is solved. They have LOTS of money. They have LOADS of money. Just let me continue. Which is why they are so 'risk-averse'. Everybody with money is risk-averse. That's why the leasing agent is 'risk-averse'. That's why Louis is risk-averse. In a way, it's a good thing... because now we know where the money is. Just let me continue. The money is wherever they won't let us have it.

JERRY: (stops) Oh for Pete's sakes. Maybe we could focus here?
> (CLAUDE frowns, like HARRY does.)
You HAVE spoken with Harry?

CLAUDE: (curt) Like I was saying, "Harry has been 'mum'."

JERRY: "Mum".

CLAUDE: But I have given it some thought.

JERRY: Yeah, I can see. Who am I talking to? What the...
> (sees CLAUDE frown like HARRY again)
...hell! am I doing? You say Harry has been "mum", and yet here you are talking to me. What is it we're doing?

CLAUDE: Walk with me Jerry?

JERRY: Are we doing laps?
   (a beat)
Look. This guy has the money. I can feel it! I mean, all you have to do is to look around, and you can SMELL it. They are not exactly eating off paper plates there.

CLAUDE: Exactly.

JERRY: Exactly?
   (sighs)
You know, you may not be Harry. But at least I have your attention. So we are in agreement here? Or not?

CLAUDE: (nodding) So he HAS to have money. You don't just assemble a fiefdom like that without some kind of wealth.

JERRY: That's what I've been saying! No, as a matter of fact, I have been SHOUTING: "We have a DEAL here folks! This guy really wants to buy something from us, right now, if not sooner! …folks." WHY won't anyone here listen to me?!!!
   (looks at CLAUDE)
Yeah, but if the leasing company can't find it...   I mean, they're like truffle pigs.

CLAUDE: That's because the leasing company isn't primarily concerned with finding CLIVE's money; they are concerned with protecting their OWN. Just as Clive is.

JERRY: ?

CLAUDE: Walk with me Jerry.

JERRY: You know, so far I'm just getting tired. I'm not getting enlightened.

   (JERRY walks with CLAUDE.)

CLAUDE: And that's because no one has yet approached this 'Clive' character and done any real selling. Just let me continue. He's been selling you.

JERRY: ?

CLAUDE: Just like Harry says! "The essence of Sales," ..err, this sale.. "is playing the ball where it lies."

JERRY: Harry said that?

CLAUDE: More or less. Just let me continue.
So what we do...

JERRY: We?

CLAUDE: Harry still gets this split if we are successful.

JERRY: (spirits pick up) Harry again, huh? Okay, shoot!

CLAUDE: We go back in there to 're-negotiate'; but instead of allowing Clive to take us to the place where he WILL sign the deal, we take him to that place where he WON'T.

      (a beat)

JERRY: Fantastic! This is brilliant! Why didn't I think of that? Hey! Maybe it's because I need half of MY brain removed. We go back in with a signed deal, and come out with an UN-signed one. This has been a great walk, you know? Call me next time you feel like stretching your legs.
And by the way, tell Harry... up yours, too.

CLAUDE: (grabbing JERRY) Because THAT's where the money is. That's where Clive keeps his OWN money. And THAT's where we begin the sale. That's where we begin the negotiations. Because it's not about the copiers; we KNOW he wants and NEEDS the copiers; it's about the FINANCING.

JERRY: You want to spin that by me again?

CLAUDE: Walk with me Jerry?

(JERRY sighs, falls in beside CLAUDE.)

SCENE 9

SETTING: That next afternoon. HARRY is cleaning out his desk, while LOUIS is in his office, looking away. JERRY and CLAUDE dance in.)

JERRY : (entering first) I HAVE FOUND GOD!!! And just when I was thinking He didn't exist…
(to ALL, as CLAUDE enters) Here's God! There He is.
          (JERRY dances around CLAUDE.)
Look at this: a $400,000. deal. Financing APPROVED.
And it's signed, sealed, "FUNDS RELEASED".
Bow down! Bow down, all of you.

BOBBY: (excitedly bowing)
(to CLAUDE) So you sniff out the money good, huh?

JERRY: So we arrive together, and Clive immediately says, "Who's this?" And I say, this is my associate Claude. "And he has some ideas about helping us find your financing Clive," I say. And instead of looking happy, he just looks suspicious.

CLAUDE: (to HARRY) Which was a good sign.

HARRY: (smiles, nods)

JERRY: "Which", as I was about to say, was a "good sign", Claude felt. And so, all the while I'm trying to talk - these two are circling.

BOBBY: (to CLAUDE) So you DO sniff out the money good, hey?

JERRY: Excuse me! But I am the one telling this story!

Hey, people! This is a BIG moment. I know you're busy, what with your proposals, and deals, and clients who won't return your calls, and the bills and frustration and the swearing and the din and all – Hey, I know you're BUSY, and it's hard! – but just give it a moment, okay? Because I think we can all SHARE in this. Because when one of us succeeds, I think the boat rises a little. We all gain, just a little! So listen up! I'm in the mood to share.

BOBBY: So... share! Where is MONEY?

JERRY: I will TELL you "where is money?" next. Okay?
    (a beat)
"Nice boat", pointing at a framed picture on the wall of this really nice yacht. "A million-five?"
(In thick, haughty British accent) "My brother's," he says.
"Nice SHELTER. ...That is, CHATEAU," Claude remarks, noticing another framed picture of this refurbished CASTLE on the wall with this JET parked in front of it.
    (joking) "Your wife's, I'll bet!"

CLAUDE: (chuckles) "Mother's," he snorts.

JERRY: (interrupting) The guy is like a billiard ball, ricocheting every direction. So I pick up the cue. "And horses... lots of them! Yours too?"

CLAUDE: We've found, by this time, that the only way to stop Clive, is to wedge him between us.

      (JERRY grabs BOBBY, so that he is between CLAUDE
      and JERRY.)

CLAUDE: (to JERRY in CLIVE's voice) "I thought you were here Jerry, to tell me that you had found the FINANCING?"

JERRY (leaning in on BOBBY) "Clive," I tell him. "One word." "Rentals."
    (BOBBY squirms.)
"It's a sweet deal. You deal directly with us, so we do an end run

around the leasing company. And, we negotiate a price you can pay."

CLAUDE: (pushing BOBBY from the other side) "And you get me the same equipment we agreed upon?" Clive asks.

JERRY: "Well, Clive. There's the rub."
     (a beat)
"You see, used machines happen to be by their very nature older. They're like divorcees with bleached hair. Still quite appealing! Hey! The sex may be just as good. But, you know, they're no longer nineteen?"

CLAUDE: "And that means?" He asks.

JERRY: "The beauty of rentals," I say, "is that if for any reason you fail to make your payments, they default to the only party who has any use for them – us."

CLAUDE: "You mean they're junk," Clive says.

JERRY: No. Not junk. But there IS a question of copy quality...

CLAUDE : ..."Ninety percent of what your associates will ever see of you is on paper. So if you don't want be found getting your paperwork confused with that of a one-man insurance agency in a tan residential office/bungalow with faded beige drapes and a wilting geranium in a transitioning neighborhood..."

JERRY: (laughs) "Who are you?" He asks again. "Claude Gustafson," Claude says! And I worked a deal with a competitor of yours, Booth Parkington of Compatible Packaging - over in Harlesburg. Perhaps you know him?"

CLAUDE: (as CLIVE) "Of course I know him. Their whole operation is running on fumes!"

JERRY: "Yeah. But he LOOKS sexy!"
     (a beat)
And he bit!

CLAUDE: Big!

(CLAUDE and JERRY do the end zone dance.)

(JERRY goes to the board and starts to add the whole $400,000. to his column.)

CLAUDE: I think he's selling one of the slower Arabians. Something about it having developed a 'cough'.

JERRY: Let's see. $400,000 plus $5,123.45...

CLAUDE: Jerry. That's TWO hundred thousand, plus $5,123.45...

JERRY: I NEVER said I'd split. I NEVER, ACTUALLY agreed to a split, with you.
I told HARRY, that IF he got it by Louis, we'd split.
And HARRY never got it past Louis, so...
        (CLAUDE grabs JERRY's tie.)
I was just letting you talk. You looked lonely.
        (JERRY gurgles.)
Some good advice, I'll grant you!

CLAUDE: Jerry. If you DON'T. do. this, they are going to find nothing but a BLOODY TURD and your bones scattered across the forest floor.

BOBBY: I think God is speaking to you, you know?

(JERRY sighs, records the split.)

LOUIS: (who has been watching this) Harry. Could I speak with you?

HARRY: (packing cardboard box) Have you noticed Louis, that I no longer work here?

LOUIS: Maybe we could talk about that.

(a long beat)
(raising voice) Maybe I could make it worth your while?

(ALL office turns to look.)

HARRY: How "worth"?

LOUIS: (looking at the board)   Let's talk.
(LOUIS sees everyone looking, while HARRY pauses to
think about it.)
Would you GET THE HELL IN HERE?

(HARRY enters LOUIS office.)

(HARRY and LOUIS meet silently, while the office bubbles
around them.)

SCENE 10

SETTING: The office, that next Monday morning. LOUIS is introducing his new sales coach, HARRY, to the "new hires".

LOUIS: The fellow I'm about to introduce – our newly created Training Director – needs no introduction. Harry's sales exploits are legendary.
I've often wished, especially at those times when things weren't going so well – I can say that now – that I wished I could clone Harry.
Well, I think I've finally figured how to do that.
Anything that Harry tells you, I want you to go home and carve into your headboards. Harry?

> (LOUIS, who has just announced the change, shakes hands with HARRY, then stands to the side, joining BOBBY, CLAUDE and JERRY.)

> (While HARRY delivers his speech, LOUIS, BOBBY, CLAUDE and JERRY all support him with comments and agreement and cheers – as if they were rooting on their favorite team.)

> (HARRY paces back and forth, stage front.)

HARRY: You ever wonder why you do what you do?
     (halts)
I hope not.
Because a salesperson knows what they want. And a salesperson works every day to get there. They're tough. And they're smart. And they work hard.

Some people may think it degrading and vulgar to sell. But I would say, look around you at this magnificent world. Everything you see is the result of someone having SOLD something, to somebody! Look in the mirror. You, yourselves, were once just a sales pitch.

(smiles with the laughter)

Life is one great sales pitch! You are the direct descents of CLOSERS.

(laughter)

And you are a small collection of the sacred few who acknowledge this.

(HARRY nods.)

People often make fun of salespeople because we look so... desperate. But life and business are conducted on an eggshell.

(HARRY acknowledges his cane.)

This is something the salesperson intimately understands, having been out and about, and done commerce with the world! A salesperson understands that all we have in this whole, cold Universe is a "Yes". And when you don't hear it, you'd best have a plan.

Well. We can live in a world where we get what we need and want at the point of a gun; that's what the government does. That's what ALL governments do. Or, we can live in a world where we get what we need and want by persuading that OTHER person that it's in their best interests we should work together freely and without animosity for the benefit of both. And that's what BUSINESS does. And THAT's sales. And THAT's our plan!

So it's a GOOD THING!!

(cheers and acknowledgement)

...which we do.

Who keeps this whole, ungainly juggernaut - this Land of Opportunity rolling? Who works hardest to stimulate the economy? Who works the hardest to bring the best and newest solutions to each and every problem? It's US! for goodness sakes. It's anybody and everybody who ever pitched anything. It's Sales People! For Pete's sakes, and SOMEBODY out there ought to be giving us a Medal.

(cheers and acknowledgement)

JERRY: I'll take it!

HARRY: Unfortunately, the only person you will probably ever hear this from is me.

> (a beat)

What you will qualify for though - if you should happen to succeed - is the respect of your peers; grand insights into human nature, and even grander hangovers! from annual award trips to the great playgrounds of this world -

> (looks around to... cheers!)

where the sun shines, and the dice roll...

> (more cheers)

and the golf balls fly, and the drinks flow....

> (and more cheers)

- to bask in the sheer joy of playing at the top of your game!

> (even greater cheers)

all the while clearing between two to three hundred thousand in yearly income!

> (loudly, encouraging their cheers)

Have I got your attention?!

> (loudest, most raucous cheering from ALL)

So let's get started! You, there.

> (ALL join HARRY stage front pointing to audience
> members.)

SELL ME A COPIER.

THE END

ABOUT THE AUTHOR

Carl Nelson spent 20 years in the Seattle theater community, during which time he wrote and produced plays, directed others, and performed whenever the talent was missing but a body still needed. Before that he did stand-up comedy. (Yes, and he also did a little copier sales.) Currently he is enjoying the obscurity of Belpre, Ohio where he writes poems that mosey about.